What Do You Do When Something Wants To Eat You?

By Steve Jenkins

HOUGHTON MIFFLIN COMPANY · BOSTON

Most animals face the constant danger of being eaten by other animals.

This book shows a few of the ways that they try to avoid this fate.

When an octopus is threatened...

it squirts a thick cloud of
black ink into the water,
confusing its attacker.

The bombardier beetle defends itself…

by shooting a mixture
of hot chemicals from
its rear end into the
face of an attacker. It
can shoot up to five
hundred times in
one second.

If a puffer fish is in danger…

it takes in water and
swells up like a prickly
balloon, making itself
almost impossible to
swallow.

The glass snake is really a lizard without legs.
When it is grabbed by the tail…

its tail breaks into many
small, wriggling pieces.

The pangolin protects itself…

by rolling into an
armor-plated ball.

The basilisk lizard is known in South America as the Jesus Christ lizard. It can escape its enemies…

by running across the
surface of ponds and
streams, using its large
feet and great speed to
keep it from sinking
into the water.

When it feels threatened, the hog-nosed snake…

rolls onto its back, sticks
out its tongue, and plays
dead. This is a good
defense, because many
predators prefer to kill
their own food.

The brightly colored clown fish escapes danger…

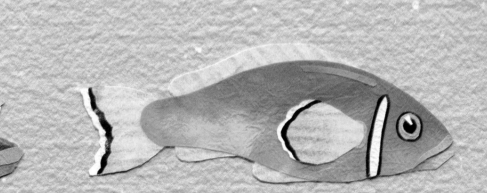

by hiding in the
poisonous tentacles of
the sea anemone. The
clown fish is immune to
the poison, but any
predator who follows is
badly stung or killed.

The hover fly is a harmless insect
without a sting. But it can protect itself
from predators…

by mimicking the
appearance of a wasp.

The gliding frog lives in trees in the forests of Asia.
It can escape predators by…

using its large webbed
feet to glide as far as fifty
feet to reach another tree.

When it spreads its wings to fly, the silkmoth…

reveals two large spots
that look like eyes on its
wings. These can startle
an attacker and give the
silkmoth time to escape.

The Javanese leaf insect looks...

almost exactly like a
real leaf. This makes it
very difficult for its
enemies to see.

The flying fish escapes danger by…

leaping from the water,
spreading its winglike
fins, and gliding as far as
a thousand feet.

The blue-tongued skink startles attackers…

by sticking out its
large, bright blue
tongue and wiggling it
from side to side.

What would
you do
if something
wanted to eat *you*?

For Alec and Page

www.hmhco.com

Library of Congress Cataloging-in-Publication Data

Jenkins, Steve.
What do you do when something wants to eat you? / written and illustrated by Steve Jenkins.
p.   cm.
Summary: Describes how various animals, including an octopus, a bombardier beetle,
a puff adder, and a gliding frog, escape danger.
RNF ISBN 0-395-82514-8 PAP ISBN 0-618-15243-1
1. Animal defenses—Juvenile literature. [1. Animal defenses.] I. Title.
QL759.J46 1997
591.47—dc21 96-44993 CIP AC

Printed in China
SCP 22 21 20 19
4500474464